Daily Devotions

First published by Parragon in 2011

Parragon
Queen Street House
4 Queen Street
Bath BA1 1HE, UK

Copyright © Parragon Books Ltd 2011
Design by Pink Creative Ltd

ISBN: 978-1-4454-3850-4

Printed in China

Daily Devotions

a collection of inspirational
thoughts and images

Bath • New York • Singapore • Hong Kong • Cologne • Delhi
Melbourne • Amsterdam • Johannesburg • Auckland • Shenzhen

To succeed,
it is necessary to
accept
the world as it is –
and rise above it.

Michael Korda

He who has a why to live can bear almost any how.

Friedrich Nietzsche

A **sympathetic** heart is like a **spring** of pure water **bursting** forth from the mountain side.

Anonymous

Only a life lived
for others is a life
worthwhile.

Albert Einstein

One man's
daydreaming
is another man's day.

Grey Livingston

Make the most
of yourself,
for that is all
there is of you.

Ralph Waldo Emerson

One life –
a little gleam
of time between two
eternities.

Thomas Carlyle

A heart in love
with beauty
never grows old.

Turkish Proverb

A man of courage
is also full of faith.

Cicero

Life is the sum of all your choices.

Albert Camus

Life is but a
thought.

Sara Teasdale

The future belongs
to those who believe
in the beauty
of their dreams.

Eleanor Roosevelt

Do not **dwell** in the past,

do not **dream** of the future,

concentrate the mind

on the **present** moment.

Buddha

You can never cross the ocean

unless you have the courage

to lose sight of the shore.

Christopher Columbus

Go confidently in the direction of your dreams. Live the life you have imagined.

Henry David Thoreau

What we see depends mainly on what we look for.

Sir John Lubbock

Your life is what your thoughts make it.

Marcus Aurelius

What humbugs we are

who pretend to live for Beauty, and never see the Dawn!

Logan Pearsall Smith

To live is so startling
it leaves little time
for anything else.

Emily Dickinson

It is not the mountain we conquer but ourselves.

Edmund Hillary

43

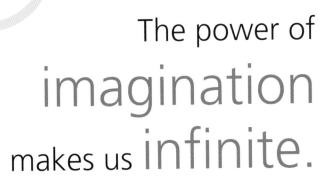

The power of
imagination
makes us infinite.

John Muir

Take time: Much may be gained by patience.

Latin Proverb

Beauty
is the promise of
happiness.

Stendhal

To unpathed waters,
undreamed shores.

William Shakespeare

Life is an adventure, dare it.

Mother Teresa

What appears to be the
end may really be
a new beginning.

Anonymous

What ever the mind of man can conceive and believe, it can achieve.

Napoleon Hill

Happiness
does not depend on
outward things,
but on the way
we see them.

Leo Tolstoy

Be kind, for everyone you meet is fighting a hard battle.

Plato

Reach high, for stars lie hidden in your soul. Dream deep, for every dream precedes the goal.

Pamela Vaull Starr

Nothing happens unless first a dream.

Carl Sandburg

Hope is faith

holding out its hand

in the dark.

George Iles

Once you choose hope, anything's possible.

Christopher Reeve

Hope is the dream of the waking man.

French Proverb

When the world says, "Give up,"

Hope whispers, "Try it one more time."

Anonymous

The soul would have

no rainbow

had the eyes no tears.

John Vance Cheney

If you spend your whole life

waiting for the storm,

you'll never enjoy

the sunshine.

Morris West

When everything seems like

an uphill struggle,

just think of the view

from the top.

Anonymous

No bird soars too high,

if he soars with his own wings.

William Blake

You never know

what you can do

till you try.

Proverb

83

Believe that you have it, and you have it.

Latin Proverb

One kind word
can warm
three winter months.

Japanese Proverb

The art of being wise is knowing what to overlook.

William James

Happiness is a grateful spirit,
an optimistic attitude,
and a heart full of love.

Anonymous

The acts of this life are the destiny of the next.

Eastern Proverb

Whatever you are

be a good one.

Abraham Lincoln

Picture credits